Retirement Savings and Investing for Beginners

Retirement Savings and Investing for Beginners

Baby Beginners *Presents*

Retirement Savings and Investing for Beginners

The Easy Way to Save and Invest for Early Retirement and Financial Freedom, No Matter Your Age

Michael Wells & Instafo

instafo

Copyright © Instafo

All rights reserved.

It is impermissible to reproduce any part of this book without prior consent. All violations will be prosecuted to the fullest extent of the law.

While attempts have been made to verify the information contained within this publication, neither the author nor the publisher assumes any responsibility for errors, omissions, interpretation or usage of the subject matter herein.

This publication contains the opinions and ideas of its author and is intended for informational purpose only. The author and publisher shall in no event be held liable for any loss or other damages incurred from the usage of this publication.

ISBN 978-1-097-26470-4

Printed in the United States of America

First Edition

Table of Contents

Chapter 1: The Importance of Retirement

1.1 Your Real Biggest Life Savings..........9

1.2 Reasons to Save for Retirement..........12

1.3 Correlation between Financial Planning and Retirement Satisfaction..........16

1.4 The Insufficient Social Security Component..........18

1.5 The Unexpected Extra Expenses..........20

1.6 To-Do: Plan for the Future Now..........22

Chapter 2: The Beginning Process

2.1 Serious Signs to Start..........25

2.2 Benefits of the Early Birds..........27

2.3 Costly Financial Behaviors During Retirement..........29

2.4 To-Do: Factors to Consider..........33

Chapter 3: Retirement Savings and Investment Options

3.1 Plant Your Money Tree..........36

3.2 401(k) Plan..........37

3.3 To-Do: Put Earnings into 401(k) Plan........................39

3.4 Individual Retirement Account (IRA)..........................41

3.5 To-Do: Invest in IRA..42

3.6 Brokerage Account..43

3.7 To-Do: Open a Brokerage Account...........................45

3.8 Micro Investing...49

3.9 To-Do: Save Up through Micro Investing.................51

3.10 Real Estate Investment...53

3.11 To-Do: Get into Real Estate....................................55

Chapter 4: Others Methods for Financial Gains

4.1 Spending Less and Cutting Back On Expenses..........56

4.2 To-Do: Track Your Expenditures..............................57

4.3 Working on the Side..59

4.4 To-Do: Take Up Freelancing.....................................61

4.5 Becoming Financially Smart......................................62

4.6 To-Do: Come Up with a Grand Budget....................64

Chapter 5: Life During Retirement

5.1 Staying Healthy Active...67

5.2 Enjoying Your Savings..70

Chapter 6: The Wisest Decision You'll Make
6.1 Final Evaluation..73
6.2 Final Thoughts...75

Retirement Savings and Investing for Beginners

Chapter 1:

The Importance of Retirement

Your Real Biggest Life Savings

Do you ever think about what it will be like to walk out the door of your job for the last time and ease into retirement life? Just imagine waking up every day leisurely without an alarm, going wherever you want whenever you want, and not having to answer to higher-up. It's the life you've always dreamed of.

But no matter how young you are, retirement will be here before you know it. And unless you start preparing *now*, you'll be working well into your sunset years in order to afford the cost of living.

We all hope and pray to live a long life, but the irony is that many people don't properly plan for their retirement years. As the old saying goes, *"if you fail to plan then you plan to fail."* So, if you aren't ready when it's time for old age and retirement, you'll have no clue what to do.

Take for instance; if you're a teenager or young adult, you already have a lot to worry about so retirement may be the *last thing* on your mind. When you do reach your golden years, you may have fewer expenses with the kids out of the house. But you'll still have bills to pay, and you'll want to have money available to enjoy life. Some people fantasize about lounging on the beach every day and sipping cocktails. The reality is, careful financial planning is very important if you wish to live your retirement years happily and achieve some of those fantasies.

On to another issue, health remains the greatest challenge most senior citizens face. As you age, your immune system gets weaker, leaving you more susceptible to diseases. It is likely that a good chunk of your savings will go towards health care.

This is why it is so important to know **how to prepare for retirement**.

Here's what you need to keep in mind: saving for retirement is different from saving up for a major purchase. Let's say you want to save enough money to buy a house. You have a specific amount in mind of how much you'll need. Once you've saved enough and reached your target, then you're basically done.

Saving for retirement is a completely different ball game because the target is <u>unknown</u>. You have absolutely no idea of what awaits you in your later years. The phrase to remember is, *"More is better."* If you think you are already saving enough for retirement, then you probably should be saving more.

But here's where things get *tricky*. Should you give up all the pleasures and conveniences in your life today and save it all for your later years? The answer is **NO**! That's because you have no idea for sure whether you'll even live into your retirement years.

Knowing how much to save – and how to save – for retirement isn't easy. But it isn't impossible. And it's not as complicated as you might think. You can save for retirement and still enjoy the luxuries of today. The <u>caveat</u> is finding the delicate **balance** between spending, investing, and saving. And we're here to help you identify your retirement saving mistakes and show you how to fix them.

Reasons to Save for Retirement

Why should you even bother to save for your retirement? Some of the reasons are the following:

1. **Life expectancy is on the rise**: According to the World Health Organization, the average life expectancy of Americans has been gradually rising over the years. Sure, there have been some slight drops from time to time. But the overall trend is upward. There are similar reports for other major countries. In fact, the average lifespan of an American is soaring up to around eighty. So, barring any unforeseen accidents *(look both ways before crossing the street!)*, you're probably going to live a long time. This means that you will need more savings to keep you going. That entails planning longer and saving more. And don't just assume you'll live to the average life expectancy age. Remember, that's an <u>average</u>. You very well may live much longer, old timer!

2. **Loss of physical and mental strength**: Have you reached that age yet where you groan a bit when you have to bend over and pick up something off the floor? If you're aren't there yet, it'll come soon enough! No matter how strong you are at the moment, you will not

be able to work forever. As you age, your physical and mental strength will begin to decline, making it difficult for you to keep up with certain tasks. A retirement fund will also make it easy for you to take a break from work. You don't want to be stuck in a "work forever" cycle, or you will never get to relax and enjoy retirement.

3. **Unpredictable problems in the future**: Whether you've had a tumultuous financial past or a pretty easy life so far, you never know what the future holds. We're sorry to be a Debbie Downer, but face the <u>facts</u>: you better not be so optimistic that you think you have – or will have – your future finances all figured out. There's no way to be sure that you will be able to save more for retirement. Think about this: there could be an unexpected crisis or emergency that will be very expensive. You must resist the urge to tap into the funds you've already saved away for retirement. It's likely that your retirement account has a penalty for early withdrawal (check with your bank, accountant, or

tax advisor to be sure), and there's a good reason for that. It serves as a good deterrent.

4. **Unreliable pension and social security**: It's true that retirement makes you eligible for Social Security and Medicare for lower-cost medical coverage. But don't rely solely on those. It's not going to be enough to live a comfortable life, and you never know when the government might change the rules. Social Security and Medicare are designed to *supplement* your retirement plans. If you have blissful retirement fantasies, Medicare and Social Security alone aren't likely to get you there.

5. **Financial burden on family**: If you have not planned your finances carefully, you fall into the risk of becoming a financial liability to your family. Imagine the extra strain on your children if they have to take care of their own children and you at the same time. This is the kind of stress that can split up families. You wouldn't want your children to avoid you, would you?

On the other hand, if you have enough saved in retirement to take care of yourself and contribute to the rest of the family, you will notice that your children will be more at ease around you. You could be one of those popular grandparents who's always giving lavish gifts to the grandkids!

Correlation between Financial Planning and Retirement Satisfaction

Does good financial planning lead to retirement satisfaction?

Retirement is often filled with unforeseen circumstances. Researchers have tried to figure out the connection between financial planning and retirement satisfaction.

One study by Rooij, Lusardi, and Alessie (www.sciencedirect.com/science/article/pii/S0167487011000195) showed that households with a long-term financial plan usually have fewer problems getting by after retirement and are in a better position to withstand unforeseen income shock.

Another study by Elder and Rudolph (https://pdfs.semanticscholar.org/adab/ef5dfc70663894c15e7277c05fd00de6c49d.pdf)
asked important questions such as whether people think about and plan for retirement, and if those who plan are more satisfied in retirement than those who did not. They tried to answer these questions using different models. In the end, their findings showed that families with higher income are more likely to be satisfied after retirement. *Makes sense, doesn't it?*

One more important finding of this research is that those who are forced into retirement by their employer or due to health-related issues are less likely to be satisfied after retirement than those who retired *voluntarily*.

Wouldn't you rather make your own decision about when to retire?

The researchers noted that this is because those forced into retirement did not adequately plan for it. The researchers noted that those who had the chance to plan in the face of forced retirement and poor health were likely to be more satisfied. These factors further highlight the urgency of starting your retirement savings on time.

The Insufficient Social Security Component

What about your social security? It may not be enough.

Social Security is calculated based on your salary history and the amount of time you spent in the workforce. In other words, it is a defined benefit plan. The Social Security calculation determines how much you will receive for the rest of your life in monthly installments, and maybe even continuing after your death.

(If you're in the United States, you can read up the full details of how it's calculated from the U.S. Government here: www.ssa.gov/pubs/EN-05-10070.pdf.)

As nice as it sounds receiving a payment each month when you retire, remember that it will be a **fixed amount,** so you won't necessarily have enough for all the unexpected expenses that come up. And spending extra for fun vacations or other nice things may not be an option for you.

Years ago, employers offered generous pension plans which were a great source of additional income for retirees. But those plans are far less common nowadays.

Remember: It's important to have multiple sources of income in retirement so you don't have to rely on a single source.

The Unexpected Extra Expenses

People who plan for retirement are usually more concerned about the big expenses like housing and healthcare. But the smaller, day-to-day expenses that build up are often ignored. In other words, don't forget the small stuff. Just when you think you have saved enough for retirement, consider the following:

Food Expense: You eat several times per day. If you're young and busy, maybe you have long stretches in between meals and snacks. But as you get older, food will likely become more of a regular routine. And that's not all. Your dietary needs will also change as you age. That extra cheese, meat-lovers pizza piled with hot peppers and onions may be your favorite meal right now. But one day your stomach will no longer be able to keep up. Also, keep in mind the difference in cost between *dining out* versus *cooking your own food*. If you prefer home cooking, you may eventually need help and will have to hire someone to cook for you. Will you have enough in your savings to put a cook on your payroll? For how long?

Exercise Routine: If you want to age gracefully, exercise should be an important part of your routine. You may need to join a gym and hire a personal trainer to guide you through appropriate exercise routines. And how will you get to the gym? We all think we are excellent drivers (Remember *Rainman*?), but someday you will have to swallow your pride and give up your keys. Hiring a driver or using other transportation options will be costly.

Retirement Home: If you are not staying with your family in your older years, it may be important to move into a retirement community where you will have companionship with people of a similar age. Some research has shown that seniors are more susceptible to depression if they are lonely. If you want to move into a retirement community, you will need to consider renting or buying a home as well as hiring in-home health care.

Entertainment Enjoyment: What do you like to do for fun? Maybe it's reading books, going to the movies, attending sporting events, or binge-watching on Netflix. We all need some form of entertainment in our lives. And when you are retired, you'll have more time available and therefore will need more entertainment options which, of course, will cost more.

Others: There are plenty of other miscellaneous expenses that you can never plan for. They just pop up and you have to deal with them. This may include personal care products, educational needs, or other expenses.

To-Do: Plan for the Future Now

After retirement, what's next? This is the single question that most people don't know how to answer. What will you be doing that will give your life meaning after you've left the workforce and are no longer driving? You might say:

- "I will play golf."

- "I will just relax."

- "I will go fishing by myself or bring along my children and grandchildren."

The truth is this: if you don't know what you want to do with your life after retirement, then you also don't know what you will need financially. You must have a blueprint of your future.

No, you don't have to have every second of every day planned out. But you can help figure out your future by answering these questions from Certified Financial Planner Michael Kay at Financial Life Focus:

1. What do you care most about?

2. Whom do you care most about?

3. What gives meaning to your life?

4. What activities would you want to explore that your current work is limiting you from doing?

As you jot down your answers, you should also think about the financial implications of these ideas. For example, if you wish to spend the rest of your life on the sunny beaches of the Caribbean, then you need to know the costs of traveling and living there, and what options are available to you. The research on this sounds simple yet is crucial: **without purpose, people do not succeed.**

Chapter 2:

The Beginning Process

Serious Signs to Start

It's never too soon to think about retirement. But, don't panic! It all depends on your age and wealth. And let's face it, your current wealth is probably the most important factor. You always have to bear in mind that a happy retirement does not just happen. You have to *P-L-A-N* for it.

Age and wealth are indeed important, but without an effective financial plan in place, many people will never want to retire because they are afraid of all of the uncertainties that will come with no longer having a job.

Retirement is one of life's major decisions, just like getting married or having children. Some people feel like they will never be ready for any of those things. But with good planning, you'll find that retirement will become a lot easier to deal with.

If you haven't really thought much about retirement planning, here are some signs that it's time to take it seriously:

Stalled Career: If you've worked in the same position for up to ten years, and you see no prospects of your career advancing any further, or your work begins to feel like a mundane routine with no challenge, you should consider retiring.

Health Priority: As we said earlier, aging comes with lots of health challenges. If you get to that point where you have difficulty with physical activities or mental stress for a prolonged period, you should consider retiring. According to the U.S. Social Security Administration (www.ssa.gov/planners/retire/retirechart.html), the earliest you can start receiving Social Security retirement benefits is age 62, but there are many varying factors.

Career Fulfillment: There is a popular saying that *it is best to leave when the stakes are high.* The career memories that you carry most profound are usually from the last thing you did on the job. When you have achieved your career goals or reached the peak of your career, it would be a good idea to retire before everything goes downhill.

Benefits of the Early Birds

We all know the cliché that *practice makes perfect*. That's what our parents, teachers, and coaches told us. The earlier you begin to plan for your retirement, the greater your chances are of being truly prepared when the time comes.

In an ideal world, you should start saving for retirement from the moment you earn your first paycheck (which is most likely not going to be anybody's case).

Wealth is not like farming where you plant an annual crop and within a few weeks it grows and bears fruit. It is better compared to perennial crops that take years to grow to maturity before you begin to reap the benefits.

The earlier you start saving for retirement, the more time you will have for your wealth to grow. The good thing is that the savings of one year will add to the gains of the next.

Take these two scenarios:

- If at age 25, you decide to put aside $3,000 per year in a tax-deferred retirement account, assuming you do that for the next ten years (until you are 35) and stop, by the time you retire at 65, your $30,000 would now be worth $338,000 if the annual return is seven percent.

- If you waited until age 35, and started saving $3,000 per year for the next thirty years (until you are 65) you would have set aside $90,000. Then, assuming a seven percent annual return, your total savings would be $303,000. Notice how that's less than the previous example where you started saving earlier and only did it for ten years.

Overall, if you should remember one thing from all this, it should be this: *the earlier you start saving for retirement, the better.*

Costly Financial Behaviors During Retirement

Many professional financial planners aren't afraid of ghosts and goblins at Halloween, but they're frightened and frazzled by fraught financial decisions that people make.

There are people out there who can't remember where their investments are or how much they have invested. *Admit it, are you one of them?* It's all about behavior.

Just to get a little off tangent here; the Centers for Disease Control says that more than one-third of Americans are obese (www.cdc.gov/obesity/data/adult.html). Some people spend tons of money on the latest fad diets, "magic" weight loss pills, and other supposedly quick weight-loss plans. *Well, guess what, tubby?* The simple solution for losing weight is to eat less and exercise more.

Similar to weight loss, so many people buy into the latest "get rich quick" schemes expecting their retirement money tree to magically sprout overnight. That's just one of the mistakes you can make that would be very costly after retirement.

Here are some other financial flubs to <u>avoid</u>:

Exceeding Expenditures: This is just basic budgeting. Let's say you earn $5,000 per month but you spend $6,000. You don't have to be a mathematician to figure out that this won't work. A lack of basic budgeting and cash flow management will make it difficult, if not impossible, to live within your means. And once you retire, you may need to be even more financially disciplined to make sure that more money is coming in than going out. *Common knowledge, right?*

Non-Existent Financial Plan: Let's say you're going to take a cross-country road trip. What's the most important thing you'll need to make sure you get to the right place? A roadmap (or these days, Google Maps). Well, you also need a good roadmap to reach your financial goals. A written financial plan should be your map and a constant reminder that will help you reach those goals. Here's a scary statistic: The Voya Retire Ready Index (http://corporate.voya.com/sites/corporate.voya.com/files/VoyaRetireReadyIndexReport.pdf) indicates that only 26 percent of retirees have a written financial plan. *Don't be one of them!*

Insufficient Saving: According to the 2018 Retirement Confidence Survey (www.ebri.org/docs/default-source/rcs/1_2018rcs_report_v5mgachecked.pdf) conducted by the Employee Benefits Research Institute, only 32 percent of retirees are very confident in their ability to live comfortably throughout retirement. Not saving enough is a huge problem as life expectancy and medical costs get higher. If you don't save enough, you won't have very many options after retirement. The Voya Retire Ready Index shows that only about one-in-three workers and retirees have a written budget or used a web-based retirement calculator. Too many people aren't saving adequately for retirement. *Sound like anyone you know?*

Abusive Credit Cards: Credit cards can be dangerous if you don't use them responsibly. Having a credit card doesn't give you carte blanche to spend. Think about the interest rate your bank pays you on your savings account. It's most likely a very small percentage. Compare that to a credit card which charges you an interest rate of 15 percent or higher if you carry a balance. Don't you see how wasteful that is? You can avoid this by only using your credit card to spend what you can pay off quickly, preferably each month. Carrying a large balance on your credit card with a high interest rate is a fool's game. *Do you feel foolish?*

To-Do: Factors to Consider

Before thinking about retirement, consider whether these three factors are vital to your retirement satisfaction:

Finance: President Franklin Roosevelt had the "three-legged stool of retirement" (www.ssa.gov/history/stool.html) metaphor in mind when he created the U.S. Social Security program in 1935. Basically, this means you will need to rely on three income sources during retirement:

1. Social Security provided by the government.
2. A retirement plan provided by your employer.
3. Your own savings.

If you haven't already done so, make a list of all your income sources and how much you make from all of them. Now look at your retirement plans and see if your income will be enough.

Healthcare: While planning for your retirement, you need to visit your physician to determine your overall health status. Of course, there may be health issues that you don't have now but will show up later in life. For example, if you have a healthy heart now but a strong family history of heart disease, then you very well may have heart problems at some point. The earlier you learn about whether you are susceptible to any age-related illness, the sooner you can begin to plan on how to manage it. With Americans living longer, you may have to consider the possibility of hiring in-home health assistance if you don't have a family to help you.

Housing/Retirement Home: If you currently rent your home, will your retirement income be enough to handle your monthly rent? Or would it be better to own a home? What about the option of joining a retirement community?

Chapter 3:

Retirement Savings and Investment Options

Plant Your Money Tree

Pay attention! Now we shall get into the meat and potatoes of it all.

You don't need to have tons of money to begin bulking up your retirement funds. You have to start somewhere, even if you are starting small.

Regardless if you think that your job doesn't pay you enough, with the right saving and investment plans, you can still have a happy retirement.

Here are the practical ways for you to start saving for retirement, ranging from the most basic to more advanced.

401(k) Plan

Do you have a **401(k)**? *Do you even know what that means?*

401(k) refers to a section in the Internal Revenue Code that deals with retirement savings contributions. Essentially, it is a tax-qualified pension account sponsored by an employer.

There are two types: the **defined benefits (DB)** and the **defined contribution (DC)**.

- In DB, the employer agrees to pay certain benefits to the employee if they meet the required criteria.

> The *benefit*, in this case, is usually calculated based on the final average salary of the employee and their services. In other words, you know what you're going to get.

- In DC, the *contribution* of the employer is defined rather than the benefit the employee will get at the end of the day. The retirement benefits are not defined in DC so you won't know in advance what you're going to get.

The employer sets up the 401(k) plan, and automatic deductions are made from the employee's salary to a tax-deferred account. Although an employee can voluntarily decide *not to be a part* of this plan, it is strongly encouraged that you join. *Why?*

There are benefits such as **investment options** and **tax deferral**. The complete list of different benefits of this plan can be found on the official 401(k) help center (www.401khelpcenter.com/401k_defined.html).

To-Do: Put Earnings into 401(k) Plan

A 401(k) sounds great, doesn't it? So here's how to get in on this action.

The first thing you need to do is find out whether your employer offers a 401(k) plan. Many employers will let you know when you apply for a job or once you are hired. You can sign up through your employer. They may ask you what percentage of your pay you would like to invest in the plan. It's common to put in about <u>eight</u> to <u>twelve percent</u>. But some experts advise putting in as much as <u>20 percent</u>. A good rule of thumb is that the more you invest now, the better off you'll be later.

By the way, depending on the amount you invest, you may be entitled to a loan from your 401(k) even before you retire. You never know when a big emergency may happen. So it's good to know you can tap into your investment if needed.

Your employer's 401(k) plan will have a minimum amount you must invest. But push your investment as high as you can.

Let's say the minimum investment is <u>10 percent</u> of your earnings. Here's how you can determine how much you can invest above the minimum threshold:

> First, you need to have a monthly budget. This will help you to determine your monthly expenses. Subtract your expenses from your earnings. Whatever's left over can go into your 401(k).
>
> For example, if you earn <u>$1,000 per month</u>, and your monthly expenses are <u>$500 per month</u>, then you'd have <u>$500 left</u>. If the minimum investment in your employer's 401(k) is <u>10 percent</u>, then that would be <u>$100 monthly</u>. You'd have <u>$400 left over each month</u>, so why not increase your monthly percentage and put more into your 401(k)?

A word of caution: Every investment carries risk, and that includes your 401(k). But the risk can be balanced by high-fund growth. If you are in your twenties, this is a great plan because you will have enough time to recover in case of a market crash, and you can rapidly grow your retirement savings.

Individual Retirement Account (IRA)

There are two types of IRAs: the **traditional IRA** and **Roth IRA**. They are significantly different in the way they operate. An IRA can be used for more investment options, unlike the 401(k). The drawback is that an IRA has a *lower contribution limit* compared to a 401(k).

- In the **traditional IRA**, you are allowed to save money that has not been taxed. In fact, Uncle Sam won't take his cut until you withdraw the money after retirement. So your money gains interest and dividends each year without being taxed.

- However, a **Roth IRA** is different. The tax is deducted from the money *before* you save. As an example, let's say you have a Roth IRA and decide to add $1,000 to it. When you make that contribution (and any other time you contribute to it), taxes will be taken out of it. But then the good news is once you retire and withdraw your money, no additional taxes will be deducted. The advantage is that you will know exactly how much you will have at retirement because the taxes were already taken out. The other good thing about a Roth IRA is that it does not restrict contributions from older workers, and there is no age barrier for withdrawal.

To-Do: Invest in IRA

If you would prefer to be in charge of your retirement, independent of your employer, then an IRA account may be your best bet.

Unlike the 401(k) where you don't really know what to expect as your final benefit at retirement, with an IRA, you will know the exact amount you have at retirement. And that makes things better when it's time to plan.

Many financial institutions offer IRA accounts. You can check with your bank online, or give them a call. Be sure to ask for all the details, including the interest rate, rules, and any penalties. It's very common for there to be a penalty if you withdraw from your IRA account before retirement.

IRAs are a low-risk, low fund investment. If you are in your early forties, this should be a better option for you.

Brokerage Account

A **brokerage** is a form of investment account. Its advantage over the 401(k) is that there is no limit to the amount of money you can save in the account.

You can still have a brokerage account while enrolled in your employer's 401(k) plan. Once you deposit any money into the brokerage account, you can use the money for investments like mutual funds, bonds, and stocks.

This diversification of savings and investment will make it easier for you to meet your retirement needs. As the saying goes, *"Don't put all your eggs in one basket."* A brokerage account also gives you the opportunity to manage your own investments.

Unfortunately, many people are just too scared to invest. And the problem is especially prevalent among younger adults. In fact, a BlackRock study (www.usatoday.com/story/money/2017/04/26/100559680) showed that nearly half of millennials say investing is *"too risky."* Don't let this fear compromise your future. Given the long-term projection towards retirement for young adults, money invested in the stock market now can grow tenfold or perhaps even more, unlike the small amount of interest you collect when your cash sits in a savings account.

Opening a brokerage account is easy, and you can do it on your own online as long as you are at least 18 years old. Once your account is set up, you will need to deposit or transfer funds into it to begin investing. There are many brokers to choose from, and you can find them by doing a Google search. Each broker has its pros and cons. Compare and figure out which one will work best for you. *This is your money that we're talking about.*

*Before you open an account with a broker, *it's very important that you know their SIPC coverage.* **SIPC** stands for the Securities Investor Protection Corporation (https://www.sipc.org). It's a federally-mandated corporation that protects you if your broker goes belly-up.

To-Do: Open a Brokerage Account

Once you open an account, the broker will ask you the kind of service you would like. There are basically two of them: **full service** and **discount service**.

- In **full service**, the broker does virtually all your investing and fund management, and they are available for you to call or visit to answer any questions you may have. A full-service broker will definitely cost you more money, depending on the specific details of the agreement.

- **Discount service** is essentially do-it-yourself. You do everything on your own, such as investing directly in stocks, mutual funds, and bonds, and you manage the account on your own.

Your choice of full service or discount service really depends on how comfortable you are with the available investment options, and how much commission you are willing to pay if you go for full service.

Some brokers also charge you even when you don't initiate transactions for a long time. You can pay cash into the account, give a check to the broker, or wire money through your bank account in order to fund the brokerage account.

Keep in mind that with a brokerage account there's no limit to the funds it accumulates, unlike a 401(k). There is also no limit to the number of brokerage accounts you can have. You can even open multiple accounts with the same brokerage firm for different **securities*** you want to acquire. Or you can open accounts with different brokerage firms to access a variety of services.

> *Don't be confused when you hear about brokerage account securities. This simply means all the *investments options* available to the brokerage accounts. They include bonds, preferred stock, mutual funds, common stock, real estate investment trusts, exchange-traded funds, money markets, master traded funds, and many more.

When it comes to buying securities through your brokerage account, there are three methods:

- The first one is called **cash service**. Here, the securities are bought using the cash you have paid into the account. Your cash should cover the value of the securities, commission, and tax.

- The second one is **margin**. Here, the broker lends you money to buy securities. You will pay him back with interest (high or low interest rate depending on the firm).

- The last one is **discretionary**. Unlike in others where you discuss with the broker before getting any security, the broker just buys for you and tells you later. This last one happens mostly in full services. You are essentially leaving the decisions up to the discretion of the broker.

If you prefer to manage your brokerage account securities on your own, the basic idea is for you to buy securities when their prices are low and sell them when the price goes up. *Common sense, huh?* This is how you make a profit in the form of interest from brokerage account securities.

Overall, once you bid your securities for sale, you will be paid before the next three working days. You should discuss all the possibilities and charges with your brokerage firm before signing up. And it's always good to consider several different firms before making your decision on which one is best for you.

Micro Investing

Thanks to technology, saving and investing don't have to be scary anymore. One easy way of saving and investing through technology is called "**micro investing**."

Micro investing is an application that gives you the opportunity to save and invest a very small amount of money each time you make a purchase. *It's very simple.*

Every time you buy something with a specific credit or debit card, the bank will *round up the bill* to the **next whole dollar**. And the extra amount is automatically deposited into your investment account.

Here's an example:

> Let's say you buy something for $29.50. The application will automatically bump up your payment to $30, and the extra 50 cents will go into your investment account. Sounds like small change when you think about a single purchase. But if you do the math, you will see how quickly these small purchases will add up over the course of a year.

The good thing about micro investing is that there is no minimum deposit amount like in most brokerage accounts. And it's an easy way for people who don't make that much money to still be able to invest. Plus there are no transaction fees.

Mirco investing is a great way for you to get into the habit of saving. Saving for retirement is a habit that should be cultivated.

To-Do: Save Up through Micro Investing

One of the most popular micro-investment platforms is Acorns (www.acorns.com). It's flexible because it rounds up your credits and debits and invests whatever is left for you. All you need to do is to sign up with the platform and provide the required details.

You can set your repeat investment to either daily, weekly, monthly, or one time depending on which you think is more convenient for you. There's also an IRA option called "**Acorns Later**."

What makes the Acorns platform more interesting is that it automatically diversifies your investment across over 7,000 stocks globally to increase the security of your investment as well as the possibility of increased return. Be aware that there is a $1 monthly fee.

Other popular micro-investing platforms include:

Robinhood: Robinhood (www.robinhood.com) offers commission-free stock trading as well as removes the three-day standard waiting time for buying and trading stocks.

ETFmatic: ETFmatic (www.etfmatic.com) is a European-based platform that allows you to easily convert savings into investments.

There are other micro-investing options out there. It's best to take a look at several of them and then decide which one is suited for you.

Real Estate Investment

Even though real estate often requires that the investor has a large amount of capital up front, it still remains a great investment option for individuals saving for retirement. Some mutual funds give investors access to the real estate sector.

Mark Hebner, the president and founder of Index Fund Advisors (www.ifa.com), said that it is better to be part of **mutual funds** or/and **Exchange Traded Funds (ETF)** than investing globally in real estate investment trusts. However, if you and your spouse earn enough to purchase real estate, then that certainly can be a great income source during retirement.

One option is to purchase a multi-family home. You and your family can live in one section and rent out the other.

The good news is that real estate *almost always appreciates*. Because the population is growing, and people are generally living longer, more people are searching for homes. It follows the basic law of supply and demand: if more people want something, and there isn't enough of it, then the price will go up.

Let's assume you bought a property when you were between the ages of 30 and 40. You should expect the value to appreciate by twice the initial price by the time you are due for retirement. You may decide to sell this property for a lump sum and use the money to buy a smaller home along the beach to enjoy that pristine view of the ocean and wake up to the chirping of birds.

Doesn't retirement sound amazing – *if you plan for it?*

To-Do: Get into Real Estate

Search for homes that are for sale in your area. You may want to get the assistance of a realtor if this is your first time and don't mind paying the commission fee.

Start with the smaller properties. If you are married or in a relationship, you can pool resources with your significant other to make your first real estate purchase. You'll likely want to research mortgage loans as well, but make sure you can pay them off quickly.

Obviously, you'll want to do thorough research on any property before buying, and that includes having it inspected. If any repairs are needed, make sure they are minimal. You don't want to buy a place that's about to fall apart. After completing any repairs, you can always rent out the home to help raise money for your next real estate purchase.

Chapter 4:

Others Methods for Financial Gains

Spending Less and Cutting Back On Expenses

Breaking Good News: You don't have to break the bank and can save money by…wait for it…*spending less*. Obviously, you don't have to be a genius to comprehend that. But it can be a toil for people to follow that such simple advice.

Think of all the things you've bought – or want to buy – that you don't really need.

For instance, when Apple introduces a new iPhone, people actually wait in line for hours so they can get their hands on a device that they most likely already have. Is it really necessary to buy the latest and greatest (and always more expensive) smartphone as soon as it goes on sale? NO!

Take a closer look at your monthly expenses and see where you *can cut back*. By chipping away here and there, you'll notice that you will have more money to save or invest at the end of the month.

As we said before, having a budget and resisting impulsive spending can be very beneficial for you. If you do a better job tracking your monthly expense, then you may be amazed at how much you really spend.

To-Do: Track Your Expenditures

There are great apps that can help you to track your income and expenditures and notify you when you are spending more than you earn.

Mint (www.mint.com) is one of the oldest but also one of the best budget-tracking applications. Look for Mint in your device's app store and install it. Once you have signed up, you can manage your money from different sources including banks, brokerage firms, credit card issuers, lenders, and other financial institutions.

There are various features on this app, but the budgeting tool is the most popular. You will need to link your credit and debit card, and the app will alert you as soon as you exceed your budget. You will also be able to see your overall cash flow at a glance. This will help you to know where your money goes at the end of the month.

There are many other budget apps available, and all of them have valuable features to help you track your expenditures. Here are a few others to take a look at:

- PocketGuard (https://pocketguard.com)

- YNAB (www.youneedabudget.com)

- Mvelopes (www.mvelopes.com)

- Wally (http://wally.me)

- Goodbudget (https://goodbudget.com)

- Personal Capital (www.personalcapital.com)

Working on the Side

Retirement doesn't actually mean you aren't working.

On the contrary, you can still work on the side after you retire. Besides the fact that it will help you earn some extra money to supplement what you already have, working on the side will help you stay active in your old age, and some scientists believe doing so can help slow down the progression of illnesses like Alzheimer's.

(We'll discuss this a little later.)

In your retirement years, you can, for example, work as a handyman, tutor, gardener, cook, etc. Generally, these are jobs that do not really have age restrictions. Helping your neighbors with their gardening or fix their broken fence will keep you active and reduce loneliness. As an added bonus, it can be good exercise. And of course, you'll make money too.

If you like to write, then blogging is an excellent idea. There are many things that you can write about: your biography, your life's mistakes, your experiences in your workplace, and your hobbies. Some of the most popular blogging platforms are WordPress.com, Tumblr.com, and Blogger.com.

Whatever job you decide to do in retirement for extra income, just remember that you don't want to do something that is so physically demanding that it will harm your health.

To-Do: Take Up Freelancing

One of the best forms of on-the-side income is to work as a freelancer. There are many people looking for freelancers with various skills, including writing, programming, designing, bookkeeping, and more.

You can sign up to be a freelancer on websites such as:

- Freelancer (www.freelancer.com)

- Upwork (www.upwork.com)

- Guru (www.guru.com)

- PeoplePerHour (www.peopleperhour.com)

- Craigslist (www.craigslist.org)

Create a free account at one or more of these sites and complete your profile, making it as polished and presentable as possible. With most of these sites, you can search for jobs based on your skill and then place a bid on the ones you think you can do. Once you are selected, you can complete the job and get supplemental earnings.

Becoming Financially Smart

Financial literacy is very important when it comes to handling money. You need to know what you're doing. Understanding the cash flow quadrant will help you determine what you need to be self-sufficient. It will guide you on how to make the most of what you have.

For example, if you spend $250 whenever you eat at an expensive restaurant *(you must have ordered the steak, lobster, and a bottle of wine!)* but discover you spend only a fraction of that when you make that meal at home by yourself, it will be easier to convince yourself that it would be better to cook your own meals. *Does that mean you can never eat out again?* Of course not. But it does mean that you should make wiser money choices overall.

By being financially literate, you will also know how to identify profitable investments and differentiate a *bad debt* from a *good debt*. That's right, not all debt is bad. If you are savvy enough, you can learn to manage your own funds and save the hundreds of dollars you would have paid someone else to do it for you.

There is still a lot of miscellanies regarding finance outside of the scope of retirement which there is no way we can cover all of them here.

If you're really a newbie, there are many specific financial classes you can take. Yes, it costs some money to take a class, but what you pay now to become financially literate is nothing compared to what you can make in the future with this knowledge.

Always be brushing up on everything there is to need to know about finance.

To-Do: Come Up with a Grand Budget

You may ask, *"How do I save more money?"* Here's how:

> 1. Make a monthly budget. Check your inflow versus your outflow. Write down all the things that you *must* pay for each month. Include all your recurring bills like water, electricity, and other utilities. Add them up and write down the <u>expense sum</u>.

> 2. Jot down all your constant sources of income like <u>your salary</u>. Include even other irregular sources of income. For example, does your Aunt Bertha send you a big fat check every year on your birthday? Add up your <u>income sum</u> and *compare it* with your expenses.

Congratulations, you just took the first step toward creating a budget.

If you are spending more than you earn, then guess what? **You are in debt!** *But don't panic.* If you find yourself in this situation, you can take action and turn things around.

1. Go back to your paper where you wrote down all your monthly expenses. Rewrite the ones that you absolutely can't live without, such as the utility bills and your monthly rent. If you realize that you've been eating out a lot, then make an effort to prepare your meals at home more often. Not only will that be less expensive, but it will likely be healthier too.

2. Look for other expenditures that can be reduced. Do you really need to pay for the fastest possible internet speed? Do you really need Netflix and Hulu? Continue to trim your expenses until your income exceeds what you spend. And *voila!* You'll be back in a positive cash flow.

Now you can put that extra cash toward some of the investment options we mentioned earlier. Go over the practical ways to save for retirement again and *choose at least two different savings plans* and follow them judiciously.

Chapter 5:

Life During Retirement

Staying Healthy Active

Many people think of retirement as a time to stop working and relax with your family, friends, or by yourself, and perhaps do some traveling you've always dreamed about.

There's nothing at all wrong with that. But you should still consider keeping your mind sharp and not allowing your body to get lazy and fragile after retirement, by continuing doing light works.

The benefits include but are not limited to the followings:

Self-Satisfaction: Immediately after retirement, you automatically have fewer things to do. You now have ample time to reflect on your life, your works, your achievements, your struggles, your friends, your bad experiences, your downfalls, your inspirations, and your strategies to fight your weakness during bad moments. *Whew,* there's a lot to think about! Looking back at all these experiences is fulfilling for any retiree. However, you will feel even more fulfilled if you use your life's experience to mentor younger people and help others grow in similar fields.

Self-Happiness: Several studies have shown that Alzheimer's may be more prevalent among those with a lower level of education and those who don't keep their mind engaged. This means one thing: the brain needs "exercise" to stay healthy. Retirees who engage in side jobs that require more of their mental input tend to stay healthier than those who do not engage in any other activities after retirement. Depression and loneliness are also a leading cause of suicide among the elderly. By going out and meeting people, you can help avoid these negative feelings. And don't forget, in addition to these scientific benefits, earning some extra cash at any age is always a source of happiness.

Self-Purpose: When you're working full time, it often feels like you're chasing the clock, especially when you balance work with family responsibilities. You barely have time for anybody except your boss and your coworkers. Then you get home at the end of the day and you are exhausted, and all you want to do is eat dinner and go to bed. You never have enough time for your children, other family, or friends. Retirement gives you the opportunity to live outside the clock. You can now relax and catch up with your social life. Retirement also gives you the opportunity to give back to society in a more profound way by volunteering. Retiring gives you a new sense of time and purpose.

Enjoying Your Savings

We've given you lots of great ideas for how to save for retirement as well as some of the benefits of retiring. But we're not finished.

Even if you do a great job saving up for retirement, once you are retired you still need to know how to spend wisely. *You don't want to squander all your savings, do you?*

All the hard work and sacrifices you made to grow your savings can be wasted if you fail to spend properly after retirement. There's no way to know how long you'll live after you retire. So you need to spend carefully to make sure you can live a comfortable life for many years after you stop working.

Here are <u>three things</u> to keep in mind if you want to spend wisely in your golden years:

Nutritious Eating: Not all foods are good for your health at the age of retirement. This may be a good time to spend more on organic food. You might want to hire a nutritionist to help you plan your meals. Consider seeing a doctor at least once a month. Your weakening immune system means you need to spot infections in time to be able to fight them properly. Regular checkups will help doctors spot any anomaly quickly and treat you effectively.

Enjoyable Vacationing: Going on vacation is good for your mental health. And retirement is the perfect time to take trips. After all those years of working and perhaps being confined to one location, now you can go wherever you want whenever you want. However, make sure you plan your vacations properly. Regardless of how much you have in your retirement savings accounts, you should still look for ways to economize your vacations. For example, you can fly economy instead of first class, and look for hotels that are offering discounts.

Healthy Exercising: Exercise is very important for your health after retirement. It helps keep you fit by taking care of your vital organs. Retirement is a great time to join a gym, and many gyms have programs and activities specifically for seniors. Don't rely solely on walking around your house briskly and strolling with your spouse in the evenings, although those are still good ways to keep in shape. You still may need an expert to determine which exercise is best for you. Working out regularly will improve your overall physical outlook. One experiment by Dr. Hideaki Soya from the University of Tsukuba in Japan showed that people who do aerobic exercise regularly such as walking briskly for about 20 minutes per day have more inflow of oxygenated blood into their brain. And that can improve your mental health. It also helps in slowing down the incidence of arteriosclerosis, diabetes, and cardiovascular diseases which can be more common among inactive people.

Chapter 6:

The Wisest Decision You'll Make

Final Evaluation

If you've made it this far, you may feel a little overwhelmed with all of the information we've provided. But don't fret. Take a deep breath. The goal of all this is to offer you solutions and options, not more worry and more problems.

Now it's time for your **final exercise**.

Having <u>one</u> or <u>two</u> savings or investment options dedicated to your retirement is enough. You don't have to take advantage of *all* the investment or saving options mentioned here.

Here is a way you can narrow your options to a few:

Are you an employee or self-employed? If you are an employee, a 401(k) would be a perfect retirement option. Ask your employer if it's available. If you are self-employed, think about opening a brokerage account or investing in real estate.

Do you have a habit of impulsive spending? You should give micro investing a try.

Take a notebook and divide the page in two. List all of your earnings on one side and all your expenses on the other side. Are there expenditures you can do without? If you get rid of those, how much will it save you monthly? On another piece of paper, make a list of the investment or saving options that are available to you. Consider the risks and returns on these investments.

What is the best investment or saving option that can accommodate the money you recovered from cutting down your expenditures?

- If you are in your 20s, you should focus on **investment options with high returns**.

- If you are in your 50s, you should focus more on **investment options with lower risk.**

Having one viable investment and retirement saving option is enough. But if you can, do more. Take it a step at a time to ensure that you're comfortable with however many routes you want to take.

Final Thoughts

Now think back to the very first question we asked: *Do you ever wonder what it will be like to walk out the door of your job for the last time and ease into retirement life?*

Retirement is a beautiful stage in life. However, the feeling can shift from sweet to sour if you fail to prepare adequately for it. The best time to prepare for retirement is when you are still young, such as in your 20s. But if that ship has sailed, then the best time to start is **<u>right now</u>**. It is not too late if you start making plans for your retirement today. The plus to starting when you're older is that you have a more solid income to invest and save with and better financial understanding to minimize mistakes than when you were younger.

There are lots of ways you can prepare for retirement, from increasing your savings to cutting down your expenses to investing in other income-generating opportunities besides your primary employment. Thanks to technology, there are lots of apps you can use to either track your cash and plan your investment.

The first step to responsible finance is having a budget. Without a proper budget, it is hard to know what comes into your pocket and what goes out. There is no way you can responsibly talk about saving for retirement if you don't know your cash flow. Once you have a concrete budget, the other parts of your retirement plans will gradually fall into place.

You wouldn't want to look back after retirement and regret the life you lived and the poor financial decisions you made.

Now you know what tools are available. There's no excuse not to get started today. Put these principles into action and prepare for your retirement. Maybe we'll see you on the beach one day!

Happy retirement!

Retirement Savings and Investing for Beginners

www.ingramcontent.com/pod-product-compliance
Lightning Source LLC
Chambersburg PA
CBHW072235170526
45158CB00002BA/901